PORTRAIT OF

Rajasthan

PORTRAIT OF

Rajasthan

MELISSA SHALES

First published in 2007 by New Holland Publishers
London • Cape Town • Sydney • Auckland
www.newhollandpublishers.com

86–88 Edgware Road, London, W2 2EA, United Kingdom

80 McKenzie Street, Cape Town, 8001, South Africa

Unit 1, 66 Gibbes Street, Chatswood, NSW 2067, Australia

218 Lake Road, Northcote, Auckland, New Zealand

ISBN 978 1 84537 763 2

Produced for New Holland Publishers (UK) Ltd by

Managing Editor **Mary Anne Evans**
Picture Research **Mary Anne Evans and Melissa Shales**
Senior Editor **Sarah Goulding**
Production **Marion Storz**
Publishing Director **Rosemary Wilkinson**

Reproduction by Pica Digital Pte Ltd
Printed and bound in Malaysia by Tien Wah Press (Pte) Ltd

2 4 6 8 10 9 7 5 3 1

COVER *The Golden Citadel of Jaisalmer is one of the oldest and most magical of the Rajasthani fortress cities, founded in 1156. Photograph © Karoki Lewis*
HALF TITLE PAGE *Rajasthani women in colourful saris during a street wedding procession, Udaipur. Photograph © Karoki Lewis*
TITLE PAGE *Detail of the Hawa Mahal, the Palace of the Winds, Jaipur, a shell building designed to capture the breeze and allow the palace women to watch the world without being seen. Photograph © Karoki Lewis*
THIS PAGE *Camels are crucial to survival in the desert, much valued and treated as part of the family. Photograph © Reuben Steains*
CONTENTS PAGE *Of all the magnificent forts in Rajasthan, Amber, near Jaipur, remains, without peer, the finest of them all. Photograph © Karoki Lewis*

CONTENTS

INTRODUCTION

RAJASTHAN

A medieval fantasy masquerading as the modern world, Rajasthan is many travellers' introduction to India, a land portrayed as something out of the *Arabian Nights*. It is an extraordinarily vivid place. Much of it may be desert but the sands are red and gold while the skies are cobalt blue, dotted by clouds of emerald green parakeets. Women dress in saris of cherry pink and canary yellow, men in turbans of orange and scarlet. The walls are painted; the floors are carpeted; the gardens are awash with flowers.

The state, on India's northwest frontier with Pakistan, was created after Independence in 1948 when the 23 Rajput rulers voluntarily gave up their kingdoms in exchange for a privy purse (later withdrawn by Indira Gandhi in 1971) linking their lands to the newly created Union of India. Rajasthan covers an area of 342,239 sq km (132,139 sq miles), with its state capital in Jaipur. It has a population of about 57 million, of whom about 90 per cent are Hindu and most of the rest Muslim. About 60 per cent of the state is part of the great Thar Desert, a ferocious environment with little rain and temperatures that swing over 50°C (122°F). Desert dwellers survive by grazing cattle, camels and goats on what little scrub they can find. The Aravalli Hills, one of the oldest mountain ranges in the world, run from the southwest to northeast of the state, offering a much kinder environment to farmers and wildlife alike.

PREVIOUS PAGE *Meherangarh Fort looms vast above Jodhpur, the most formidable of all the ancient city palaces of Rajasthan.*

BELOW *Travelling alone as a woman introduces a whole new aspect of India. Few Indian women will approach Western women who are in a group or with a man, but if you are alone, you will be adopted wherever you go, finding the life of laughter and tears beneath the vivid silks of the Rajasthani women.*

RIGHT *Rajasthani men take their turbans to extremes, vast swathes of brightly coloured cloth, up to 18m (60ft) long, tightly wound in up to 1,000 different styles. The colour, style and type of cloth can all denote the caste of the wearer and will also vary according to the season and for different events, such as weddings and funerals.*

Rajasthan never came under the direct rule of either the Moghul Emperors or the British, with the Maharajahs signing treaties with both great empires that left them in day-to-day control of their own lands. As a result, the feel of the region is extremely different to most of the rest of India. The area is significantly poorer, with little major development, and low levels of education, health care and women's rights. On the plus side many of the artistic and architectural glories that were pre-British India have survived longer here, and the way of life, while distinctly less comfortable for the local people, is undoubtedly far more colourful for the visitor. There are plate glass windows and air-conditioned taxis, but you are just as likely to be sharing your traffic-jam with a camel cart or doing your shopping at a tiny stall, where a man on a rickety stool makes the slippers he sells. The air is streaked by the smell of car exhausts and sewers, jasmine and turmeric. Cows wander placidly through the traffic, ignoring the squeal of horns and brakes. Oxen are yoked to the lawnmowers and water buffalo paddle in the muddy shallows near where the boys are bathing in the lake. Great festivals are celebrated with colour and light, camel races and elephant polo, pilgrim chants and gypsy dances.

LEFT *The sleepy lakeside town of Pushkar is a major pilgrimage centre, home to one of only two temples in India dedicated to Lord Brahma. Every autumn, for twelve days, it erupts in the Pushkar Mela, one of India's best known and most colourful festivals.*

Rajasthan survives on tourism, depending on its fabulous cultural, architectural and natural heritage to bring in the steady stream of visitors that supply its hotels and tour companies, use its transport and restaurants, buy its handicrafts, help restore its crumbling monuments and preserve its natural environments. Most tourism is city-based, in the old historic capitals such as Jaipur, Udaipur, Jodhpur and Jaisalmer, but more and more people are heading to smaller towns such as the enchanting painted towns of the Shekhawati region, to Bundi and Kota in the southeast, and the hill station and pilgrimage centre of Mount Abu in the southwest. Numerous small forts, palaces and hunting lodges are being restored as charming heritage hotels, often offering a variety of activities from village safaris to camel or horse trekking in the desert. The Palace on Wheels takes the luxury track around the state, with guests sleeping in coaches fit for a maharajah and cosseted within an inch of their lives. There are several fine wildlife reserves, at Ranthambore, one of the last remaining tiger reserves, Sariska, and the Keoladeo Ghana bird sanctuary in the former hunting grounds at Bharatpur where the dawn will bring the call of an ibis or the low growl of a hunting cat.

Building Paradise in the Desert

Throughout history, bloodshed and beauty have walked hand-in-hand. In Rajasthan, the warrior princes created a vision of paradise in stone. There are formidable fortresses such as Jaisalmer, Jodhpur and Kumbhalgarh whose hefty walls scream defence, but within them the architects used an astonishingly delicate touch. High ceilings and cool corridors carry away the desert heat. Jaali screens of carved stone allow the light and breeze in without obstructing the view, protecting the privacy of the watcher at the window. Walls are painted with a tracery of flowers, stirring battles or tender love scenes, or even with a steam train or bi-plane. Mirror mosaics reflect the candlelight a thousand-fold and in the paradise garden outside, cooling rivulets of water run between perfumed flower and fruit trees. More than all the stone, this is the real ostentatious wealth of Rajput building, precious water displayed for entertainment in a barren land.

LEFT *The view across Bikaner from the Maharajah's private apartments, Junagarh, built in 1588 by Maharajah Rai Singh, one of Moghul Emperor Akbar's generals.*

TOP RIGHT *Sunrise over the Fateh Prakash Palace, Shiv Niwas Palace and the City Palace, in Udaipur. One of the newest and most beautiful cities in Rajasthan, its cool white buildings are built on a cascading series of lakes.*

BOTTOM RIGHT *The late afternoon sun glows over Jaisalmer, the golden fort that grows organically from the desert rock.*

LEFT *On a limestone platform surrounded by giant stone elephants, the Jag Mandir lies on an islet at the southern end of Lake Pichola in Udaipur with magnificent views across the Lake and City Palaces. Built as a royal guesthouse in the late 16th century, Moghul Emperor Shah Jahan stayed here in 1623–24 while leading a revolt against his father, Jehangir. It is said that he was so taken by its intricate decoration that it was one of his inspirations when he later built the Taj Mahal.*

TOP RIGHT *Local artists chose anything around them for inspiration, such as this 19th-century mural of a European lady operating a sewing machine at Rathi haveli in Laxmangarh, Shekhawati.*

BOTTOM RIGHT *The Ganesh Pol, Amber Fort, is decorated inside and out, its delicate lattice-work jaali screens interspersed by painted flowers.*

LEFT *Tourists are not the only ones to spend their days wandering the streets; this cow seems equally taken with the architecture of Jaisalmer.*

ABOVE *Between welcoming tourists, attendants still serve the Maharajah, who retains rooms in Jaipur's City Palace.*

RIGHT *It can take time to adjust to life in India, but the more you embrace the local lifestyle, the easier it becomes. Take to the streets and this difficult but vibrant society captures your heart.*

OVERLEAF *The shaded courtyard of a darga (Sufi mosque and tomb).*

THE MAHARAJAHS

In Sanskrit, the word *Rajput* means 'son of a king'. The early origins of the Kshatriya (warrior) caste who colonized northwest India from the 7th century onwards lie in the Turkic tribes of Central Asia and Afghanistan. Legend divides them into the suryavanshi (solar) clan, descended from Lord Rama, hero of the Ramayana; the chandravanshi (lunar) clan, descended from Krishana, hero of the Mahabharata; and the agnikula clan, born from the sacred flames of Mount Abu. These three clans were subdivided into 36 races and 21 kingdoms, of whom a few rose to greatness. The Sisodias settled in the Aravalli Hills in the 7th century, first at Chittorgarh then Udaipur. The Rathores moved into the region from Uttar Pradesh in the 14th century, ruling the kingdom of Marwar from Jodhpur. The Kachhwahas came west from Gwalior in Madya Pradesh in the 12th century, settling at Amber then Jaipur. Over to the west, the Bhattis built their desert fortress at Jaisalmer in the 12th century. The Chauhans ruled Ajmer, Bundi and much of Shekhawati.

LEFT *By the 16th century, the Moghuls were the Imperial overlords of the Rajput princes and many of the lotus-eating practices of the Moghul court, as shown in this Moghul miniature, were eagerly adopted by the Maharajahs.*

TOP RIGHT *A group of Rajput princes pose in the baithak (reception room) of the Sneh Ram Ladia haveli in Mandawa, Shekhawati.*

BELOW RIGHT *Mural of Sardul Singh (Rao Shekha's son) dividing up Shekhawati kingdom between his five sons. From the upper room of the abandoned Chaudhri haveli in Fatehpur, Shekhawati.*

The Early Years

Known above all for their valour, their chivalry and their honour, the Rajputs were renowned warriors, feared in battle but hampered by one major flaw. Although they had a common heritage and ethos, they were never able to live together in harmony. Instead they spent the centuries squabbling amongst themselves, unable to work together even when faced by a formidable common enemy such as the Delhi Sultans or Mughal Emperors. Some married into the Delhi court and ended up leading the Muslim armies against their fellow Rajputs, having wealth showered upon them as a consequence. Others held out beyond all hope. Every battle was hard-fought, while death was chosen time and again in preference to defeat. Story after heart-rending story tells of *jauhar* – the mass suicide of the women and children in a city facing surrender – while the men rode out in one last, hopeless charge to face certain death. Each time, thousands died, but somehow someone lived to tell the tale and rebuild the state ready for the next bloody battle.

This all made Rajput history stirring and sorrowful but also extremely complicated, and for all the to-ing and fro-ing, relatively little changed over the centuries. The ruling classes concentrated on fine art and fighting, living on taxes and the profits of war, while the merchant classes traded with the passing camel trains and the poor were left to get on with surviving as best they could while being taxed by absolutely everyone.

There were 23 separate kingdoms in Rajasthan. Sometime in the early 19th century, they all made deals with the British, finally bringing to an end the cycle of bloodshed, and from then on the various rulers became more and more taken with the good life, a situation encouraged by the British who quietly got on with running their country for them.

RIGHT *The sun sets over Chittorgarh Fort. This vast complex, founded in the 7th century AD, sprawls over a 283 ha (700 acre) hill near Ajmer in southern Rajasthan. It was the capital of the Sisodia clan of the Rajputs from the 8th to 16th centuries. During this time, it was sacked three times, each time its rulers leading the entire population in a mass suicide or jauhar rather than submit to foreign rule. On the third occasion, in 1568, Maharajah Udai Singh II survived, reestablishing his rule in Udaipur.*

Life at Court

The Rajputs had a clear sense of their own identity but they never hesitated to borrow trends from those more successful. While both the fabric and lifestyle of the palaces and forts adhere to the Hindu tradition, both also show clear Muslim and British influence, whether in the shape of a dome or the Rolls Royce stabled next to the elephant. Walk around the palace museums in Jaipur, Jodhpur, Bikaner and Udaipur and you soon get a sense of the opulence of life at one of the great royal courts, where money flowed more freely than water and life was designed to be sweet, with fabulously decorated rooms surrounding courtyard gardens cooled by fountains. The maharajahs indulged their passions freely, from hunting to collecting, but while the men played, the women lived a far more constrained life in the *zenana* (harem), expected to be beautiful, noble, valiant and courageous, to have absolutely no say in their own affairs during their lives and die with dignity at their husband's or master's side. Servants were, effectively, invisible people.

ABOVE *Sati hand prints at Meherangarh Fort, Jodhpur, each denoting a wife burned on her husband's funeral pyre.*

TOP RIGHT *Palanquin, used for carrying the royal family around the streets of Jodhpur, displayed in Meherangarh Fort.*

BOTTOM RIGHT *Detail on Tripolia Gate leading to the City Palace, Jaipur, showing the Kachhwaha ruler of Amber Sawai Jai Singh in the early 18th century.*

FAR LEFT *One of the two gangajali, the largest silver vessels in the world, used by the Maharajah of Jaipur to carry Ganges water on a visit to England in 1902 so he would not lose caste by drinking impure English water. Each weighs 345 kg (762 lbs).*

LEFT *An ancestral maharajah stares stony-faced at the tourists delighting in his hospitality at Neemrana Fort, now a heritage hotel.*

LEFT *The Hawa Mahal (Palace of the Winds) is perhaps the most famous building in Rajasthan, designed to let the ladies of the court watch the outside world in comfort without being seen. It stands at the front of the Chokri Sarhad (City Palace), which covers two of Jaipur's nine city blocks. Jaipur is known as the Pink City, its already reddish city and palace walls painted a deeper ochre red in the 19th century. The colour is considered to be a sign of hospitality.*

The Modern Maharajas

Following Indian independence, all 23 Rajput principalities voluntarily joined the Union. In 1949, the Maharajahs gave up their power and lands, retaining their titles and a privy purse. Many promptly stood for parliament and went on to win their local constituencies. Others took their social skills and contacts into diplomatic circles or have become industrialists. These days, they have no political power, but they still have enormous influence and standing in the local communities and continue many of the charitable and public works that were once part of their duties. Even a minor member of the royal family visiting rural villages is still likely to be met by praise singers who will extol the virtue of his ancestry as he walks through the streets. Most retain apartments in the royal palaces and live a jetset lifestyle with Rolls Royces and Bentleys to replace the elephants, and apartments in London and the south of France. Many are also turning to tourism, with their palaces flourishing as heritage hotels. These days, however, their status as 'modern maharajahs' is being usurped by the flourishing Indian financial moguls who have made their money in silicon and are buying their way to opulence and indulgence.

BELOW *Tourists enjoy the Chess Dance on the roof of the Taj Hari Mahal hotel in Jodhpur, a former palace.*

TOP RIGHT *Surinder Singh and son in the Shahpura Fort, Shekhawati. Converting old family properties into hotels is a way of financing restoration.*

BELOW RIGHT *Polo was invented on the sub-continent while the famous riding trousers come from Jodhpur.*

TAG Heuer
3
6
6½
Hindustan Times
Because you deserve to know
RAJASTHAN POLO CL
HT Jaipur Live
Indian Airlines

The Wedding

Times are changing, but arranged marriage is still prevalent at all levels of Indian society. In Rajasthan, once the match is set, the parents' horoscopes are compared by a priest and if compatible, a coconut is exchanged to seal the deal. Families are frequently plunged into terrible debt by the cost of the festivities and the dowry which must still accompany their daughter to her new home.

Wedding ceremonies have, in some cases, shortened from the spectacular five-day feasts that were the norm at all levels of society, but a Hindu wedding is still always a magnificent event. The formalities begin a couple of weeks before the actual ceremony, which is traditionally conducted in Sanskrit. Engagement ceremonies are held at the separate family homes. Gifts are exchanged and the bride and groom are anointed with uptan, a paste of sandalwood, turmeric and rose water. The groom then processes, on horse, camel or elephant, to the home of the bride, where vows and offerings are made to the sacred fire. The couple are generally given money by guests to help them set up their new home and the feasting and dancing goes on for days. The Rajput wedding creates a formal link between the two families which lasts for seven generations.

BELOW *A Brahmin priest conducts the traditional Hindu wedding ceremony of the Maharawal of Jaisalmer, Brijraj Singh, and his Nepali bride in New Delhi.*

RIGHT *Women family members wash the feet of the couple during the wedding.*

OVERLEAF *The City Palace in Udaipur is actually a whole complex of palaces built by different rulers over a 400-year period.*

ARCHITECTURE

There are simply not enough superlatives to cover the magnificence of the architecture in Rajasthan. At village level, houses are humble to the point of being shacks, but those with money chose to trumpet their achievements in stone, from the powerful fortress walls of early Kumbhalgarh and Chittorgarh to the filigree finery of Jaisalmer or Amber. The merchants' havelis of Shekhawati were painted from top to bottom, while later rulers in Jaipur and Udaipur borrowed from the Moghuls to create harmonious palaces with fountain courtyards and paradise gardens. Out of town, the princes built themselves hunting lodges and pleasure playgrounds, such as the Monsoon Palace at Deeg, with its elaborate fountains. In this land where water is treasured, even wells and tanks (reservoirs) are works of art. Religion has also left its stamp on the landscape. Much of the early Hindu architecture was eradicated by the arrival of Islam, but a wave of temple building from the 8th–11th centuries AD created many masterpieces such as the Jain temples in Chittorgarh, Jaisalmer, Mt Abu and Ranakpur, decked from top to toe in elaborate and intricate carvings.

PREVIOUS PAGE *Amber Fort reflected in Maota Lake.*

BELOW *Junagarh in Bikaner is the only major fort in Rajasthan never to have been conquered, part of the reason for the perfect condition of its exquisite stonework.*

RIGHT *Golden Jaisalmer appears to have been crocheted rather than built, every window designed as a perfect frame, every wall a work of art.*

Jaipur

Now the state capital of Rajasthan, Jaipur is a relatively new city, custom-built as a capital by Maharajah Jai Singh II of Amber in 1727 and designed by Bengali architect, Vidya Bhattacharaya, based on ideal Hindu principles of architecture, laid out in a treatise called the *Shilpa-Shastra*. Two of the nine blocks were taken for the City Palace, which today houses a fabulous museum, offices and the Maharajah's private apartments. Various nobles and tradespeople were invited to build on the others, with each area set aside for a different trade. It is one of the most visited cities in India, with tourists drawn by its rich pink walls, wealth of palaces and mansions, and fabulous shopping and crafts. In the area immediately around the city are many other magnificent monuments such as the extraordinary Jantar Mantar, Kings and Queens' Gaitors (tombs) and the modern Lakshmi Narayan Temple.

BELOW *The courtyard of the City Palace, Jaipur, showing the back of the Hawa Mahal, the Palace of the Winds, a cool discreet place from which the palace ladies could watch the activities in the Johari Bazaar below.*

TOP *A Diwa Burj (watchtower) at the Jaigarh Fort, perched high above Amber. It takes some effort to get up here but the views are incomparable, one of the reasons it was a key lookout point for the whole state.*

BELOW *A tour guide explains the workings of a sun dial at the Jantar Mantar, Sawai Jai Singh's fabulous astronomical observatory, started in 1728. It has 18 instruments which can calculate the time, date, season, monsoon and signs of the zodiac as well as plotting the movement of the sun, moon and stars.*

Amber Fort

The last and largest of a long line of forts constructed in these hills by the Kuchhwaha family since the 11th century, Amber (pronounced Amer) was built in 1592 by Maharajah Man Singh, who had been brought up at the Moghul court and became Commander-in-Chief of Emperor Akbar's army. The close family connection brought vast wealth and privilege and the fortified palace shows strong elements of Moghul design. The fort is built in four sections. Some parts are now ruinous, but well over half of the complex is still magnificent. Some of the highlights include the Shila Devi Temple with its vast silver doors and temple lions, the Ganesh Pol, the elaborate gateway to the Maharajah's private apartments, and the extraordinary Sheesh Mahal (Hall of Mirrors), inset with hundreds of thousands of glittering shards of glass.

BELOW LEFT *Along the outer walls, windows were positioned to make the best of both the breeze and the view.*

TOP RIGHT *The view along the vast exterior walls of Amber Fort to Amber Village below and the Aravalli Hills beyond.*

NEAR RIGHT *The complex delicacy of the painted ceilings dazzles and delights.*

FAR RIGHT *The main entrance courtyard, Jaleb Chowk, is where returning armies would display their booty to the population. Now it's where you catch your elephant for the trip down the hill.*

Jodhpur

Jodhpur was one of the greatest of the Rajput kingdoms, its rulers claiming descent back to the sun itself. The founder of the kingdom, Rao Singh, arrived in the desert in 1182; Rao Chunda conquered Marwar in 1381 and his grandson, Rao Jodha, moved his capital to clifftop Jodhpur in 1459. The Marwaris are great traders and the city grew fat on the trade along the Silk Road, signing a highly profitable treaty with the British as early as 1818. But they also had a bloody history and the heavily fortified citadel was more than a conceit. The city walls are 10 km (6 miles) long and up to 45 m (148 ft) high. A road winds up the 125 m (410 ft) cliff through seven gates, each sufficient to stop a charging elephant. The latest palace, added in 1853, is lavishly decorated with marble and sandalwood, painting and gilding. It also includes a fine collection of furniture from children's cradles to elephant howdahs and campaign tents used by Emperors Shah Jahan and Aurangzeb. Beyond the citadel, the city is best known for its sea of blue houses, but it is also worth visiting the vast, slightly gloomy Umaid Bhawan, built by British architect HV Lancaster between 1929 and 1943 as a famine relief project. This was the last royal palace ever built in Rajasthan and it is now a luxury hotel. The Maharajah maintains apartments here.

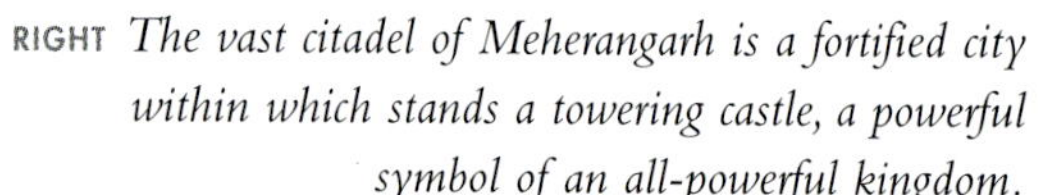

RIGHT *The vast citadel of Meherangarh is a fortified city within which stands a towering castle, a powerful symbol of an all-powerful kingdom.*

LEFT *Blue is the colour of the Brahmin caste and the blue houses below the fort in Jodhpur denote a Brahmin (priestly, high caste village). However, the colour is also said to fend off mosquitoes and flies and help cool houses, both highly useful properties.*

Udaipur

It may look like a perfect landscape, but nothing in Udaipur is natural – even the lakes are constructs, a cascade of dams created within the folds in the hills and then as carefully decorated as a wedding cake – and to much the same effect.

Udaipur is delightful, a blue and white confection of a city founded by Maharana Udai Singh in 1568 after he and his surviving people had fled from Chittorgarh. Its peaceful appearance belies a history that continued to shed blood until a treaty with the British provided protection in the 19th century.

The main town clusters round the lower lake, Lake Pichola. The shoreline is dominated by the vast City Palace, entered through the Tripolia Gate where the Maharana would have himself weighed and distribute his weight in gold and silver to his subjects. Other smaller palaces and mansions line the shores, and in between are bathing ghats and cupolas. On the hill above is the Sajjangarh (Monsoon Palace), but look out into the middle of the lake for the sheer, gloriously romantic frivolity of the Lake Palace, now a luxury hotel.

BELOW *A symphony of blue and white, the Lake Pichola waterfront has a harmony and elegance totally unlike anything else in India.*

RIGHT *The Taj Lake Palace has become a global icon, seen as Octopussy's lair in James Bond and in countless fashion shoots.*

BELOW RIGHT *The bathing ghats beneath the Bagore-Ki-Haveli, a waterfront palace built in the 18th century by Amir Chand Badwa, the Prime Minister of Mewar.*

Jaisalmer

The Yadav Bhatti Rajputs were renowned medieval warriors who moved south from the Punjab to set up this distant, dusty kingdom. In 1156 the sixth ruler, Rawal Jaisal, moved his capital from nearby Lodrhuva, building himself a new fort, the Sonar Quila (Golden Fort) from the local sandstone. Its fat, round bastions crown 80 m (262 ft) Trikuta Hill. As with all the desert kingdoms, the Bhatti lived a bloody life, scrapping with their neighbours (mainly Jodhpur and Bikaner) over scarce water and cattle. But Jaisalmer also grew prosperous as a key staging post on the camel caravans that linked India to Egypt, Arabia, Persia, Africa and the West. In 1294 Emperor Ala-ud-din Khilji grew so furious at the high level of the taxes demanded that he besieged the city for seven years before the women finally committed *jauhar* (mass suicide) and the men dressed in saffron and rode out of the gates for the final confrontation.

Fortunes continued to fluctuate according to whether the state was in favour with the emperors, until Jaisalmer signed an accord with the British in 1818. Within the sturdy walls is one of the most magical collections of buildings in India, with the royal palace and magnificent havelis built, largely by Muslim craftsmen, for wealthy merchants and the local aristocracy, such as the 17th century Salim Singh Ki Haveli and 19th century Nathmal Ji Ki Haveli and Patwon Ji Ki Haveli, all intricately carved and decorated from top to bottom, inside and out. Matching them, detail for detail, are seven exquisitely ornate Jain temples. Outside the walls, Gadsisar Lake, a precious 14th century rainwater reservoir, is surrounded by small temples and shrines.

Although the buildings are protected, the fort is very much alive, with over a third of the town's population still living within its walls.

RIGHT *The most isolated town in India, miles across the desert on the Pakistan border, Jaisalmer seems to materialize from nowhere under floodlights.*

LEFT *Several of Jaisalmer's old havelis have been converted into heritage hotels, offering stylish accommodation with stupendous views.*

RIGHT *Within the fort walls, most of the town of Jaisalmer is as delicate as gossamer, every inch of stonework on the havelis (merchants' houses) intricately carved in lacy designs. This exquisite balcony is just one of many.*

BELOW RIGHT *Elephants are considered to be symbols of good luck and prosperity in Indian culture, a fitting symbol to stand outside the Nathmal Ki Haveli in Jaisalmer, the former home of a Prime Minister.*

Havelis

Taken from the Persian word for 'an enclosed space', the havelis were merchants' houses in north India and Pakistan, built in the Islamic style and usually dating from around 1830–1930. Typically, a haveli has two courtyards, one with public access and one for the women, although the largest may have up to four courtyards and three storeys. Around the courtyard a colonnade will provide shade and access to the rooms. There are havelis in every city in Rajasthan, but those within the citadel in Jaisalmer are particularly noted for their elaborate stonework. If you want to see the art of the haveli in its finest form, travel to the Shekhewati region in northeastern Rajasthan, where the Marwari traders commissioned ever more elaborate monuments to their own financial prowess.

Not only were they magnificent buildings, but artists were commissioned to paint them inside and out with scenes from mythology, history, and everyday life. Krishna may cavort with his milkmaids next to a Victorian lady with a sewing machine; Moghul emperors gallop to the hunt past a steam train. Sadly, while some have been rescued as hotels, many have sunk into slums.

BELOW *Lucky elephants and dancing girls flank this painted doorway in Mandawa, one of the most interesting of the towns in the Shekhawati region with frescos that range from the Wright brothers to erotica.*

TOP *This opulently decorated room in the Hukmichand Sagarmal Chaudhri Haveli, Fatehpur, is one of the few to have been restored to its original glory, giving a true idea of the lavish colour and design that once covered much of the Shekhawati region.*

BELOW *At the other end of the scale, sights such as this abandoned Chaudhri haveli in Fatehpur are all too common. Its doors and windows have been ruthlessly ripped out by unscrupulous antique traders. The rooms upstairs still contain some of the finest murals in Shekhawati, but it is only a matter of time before the whole building collapses.*

ARTS & CRAFTS

Jaipur may well be the craft capital of the world, a shopper's paradise of lavish beauty whether your budget is pennies or pounds. It is the jewel in the crown of a state that has decorated itself from top to toe and intends to do the same for all its visitors. Rajasthan is one of the world's largest centres for hand-cutting gems and a great place to buy rubies, emeralds, and sapphires as well as lesser stones such as topaz or carnelian, which can be set to your own design or in exquisite traditional styles. Heavy tribal silversmithing and gleaming glass and lac bracelets (said to be good luck) provide personal adornment at a lesser cost. Buy lovely silks and get a local tailor to make up clothes to your own design, and add elaborately patterned jooties (slippers) and bags. For the home, there are block print and tie-dye cottons and silk cushions and curtains, pretty blue and white Jaipur pottery, camel-hide lampshades from Bikaner, white marble and pink and green soapstone, enamelled silver and brasswork, carved and inlaid wood and miniature paintings, based on very distinctive local regional traditions. And finally, set it all off with a traditional rug or cotton or camel-hair dhurrie, rescued from its origins as underlay to take pride of place on your hearth.

BELOW *Block print tablecloths and bedspreads are a cheap, colourful and attractive souvenir, the traditional floral and geometric patterns reproduced in rich natural dyes.*

RIGHT *Silk is deliciously cheap in Rajasthan, and it is possible to get cushions and curtains, or even to take a pattern and get an evening dress made to your own design.*

BELOW *Everything in Rajasthan is decorated, even the elephants. Before going to work at Amber Fort, this particular beauty queen had a full facial, make-up and even pedicure.*

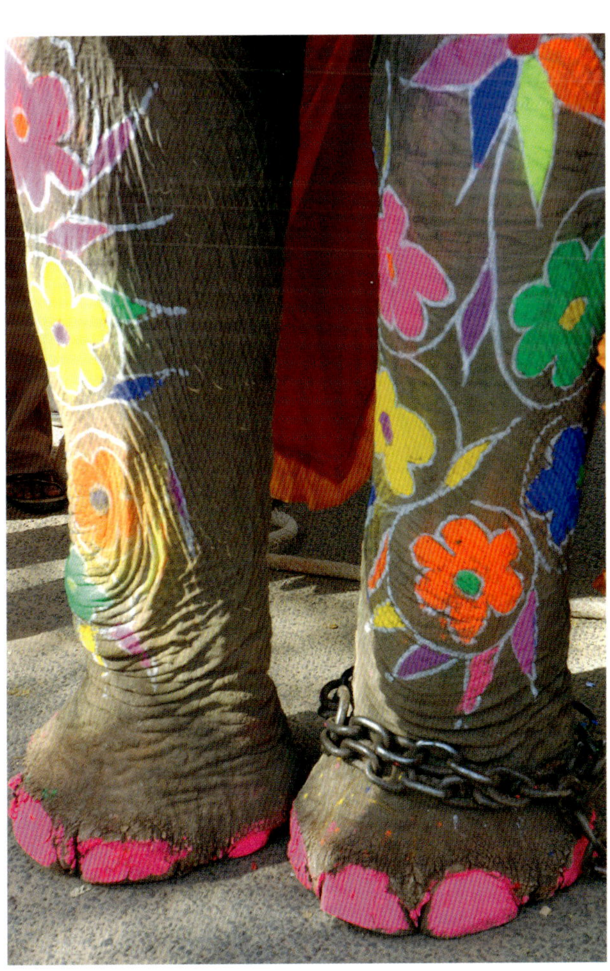

TOP LEFT *Block printing is a simple process which starts with a length of cotton cloth and wooden stamps, many of which have been used for decades. Typically, two or three colours are used in the design.*

BELOW LEFT *Women put the finishing touches to a traditional dhurrie. Their simple geometric designs and muted colours are popular with the western market.*

TOP RIGHT *Many of the carpet shops are also factories that offer tours and demonstrations of how the carpets are made. Unusually, a man is at the loom. More frequently the work is done by younger women, whose nimbler fingers are better suited to the task.*

BELOW RIGHT *Buying your textiles can be performance art, with flourishes, haggling, plenty of tea and an Aladdin's cave of beautiful fabrics, all screaming 'buy me'.*

ABOVE *A jewellery maker with a blowtorch in Jaipur. Traditional kundan and minakari styles back gemstones with exquisite gold and lacquer settings.*

LEFT *Marionettes (kaputlis) are an old Rajasthani art form, made with a brightly painted wooden head and a roughly formed soft body that can then be clothed in a variety of costumes made by the puppeteers.*

RIGHT *Like many rural women, this Rajasthani girl at Kelvara village, near Kumbhalgarh Fort, wears the family fortune in elaborate silver jewellery.*

ENTERTAINMENT

Rural Rajasthan remains extraordinarily rich in local music and dance, with many instruments found nowhere else in the world. Musicians wander the fairs and city streets; village women sing ballads about water and skirmishes with their mothers-in-law, and the men answer with stirring songs of heroism in battle. Bhil women circle together, skirts billowing in the *ghoomar*, and with the men in the *gair ghoomar*, the only dance danced by both sexes together and then only during the Holi Festival. Even to this day, travelling storytellers use props such as puppets or the kavad, an unfolding painted cartoon box, to tell stories such as the Ramayana or epic exploits from Rajput history to enthralled audiences in remote villages. Although these days, they may also be talking about best agricultural practice – the government uses old methods to educate the illerate villagers. Added to this rural richness is the legacy of royal patronage that gave the wow factor to the travelling players. These days, almost every hotel presents spectacular live performances for its guests, as magnificently costumed women balance piles of pitchers on their heads or dance on sword blades in the *bhavai* while men perform dazzling acrobatic feats, fight on dummy horses in the *kachhi ghodi* or walk in a trance across blazing coals.

RIGHT *There is still a strong tradition of tribal dance in Rajasthan with wandering troupes who visit the fairs and festivals. Many of the dances and the instruments that accompany them are found only in the state.*

TOP *Indian classical dance grew out of a tradition of temple worship. It is a subtle art, full of tiny, precise gestures and glances that can be read like a book.*

RIGHT *Every tourist hotel lays on displays of dance, some from the local area, some picking up dances from across the sub-continent.*

TOP LEFT *Wandering minstrels pop up everywhere from street corners to the hotel breakfast room. Keep plenty of small coins handy.*

BELOW LEFT *Nomadic puppeteers have been a part of Rajasthani tradition for centuries, entertaining court and commoner alike with flamboyant shows that can involve acrobatic stunts, flaming torches and great religious and heroic epics.*

TOP RIGHT *Bollywood may be based in Mumbai, but Rajasthan, like the rest of the Indian world, is hooked on its movies, with their swashbuckling charms and song and dance, where good triumphs, the boy gets the girl and the finale is fun.*

BELOW RIGHT *A cut above the average recreation – elephant polo entertains those having tea on the lawn at the Taj Rambagh Palace Hotel, Jaipur.*

FOOD

Several key factors have coloured Rajasthani cuisine – a lack of water and firewood, the almost constant state of warfare that necessitated dishes for armies on the move, and the state's extraordinarily rich royal heritage that not only borrowed from British and Moghul cuisines, but based food fit for kings on a dozen different local traditions. Many traditional Rajput dishes will survive long periods in the intense heat and can be eaten without reheating. There are relatively few fresh vegetables, but plenty of pulses. Ghee (clarified butter) or buttermilk is generally used instead of oil, and cracked wheat instead of rice. In Maheshwari cooking, powdered mango takes the place of tomatoes and asafoetida replaces garlic and onions, which were difficult to find in the desert and were considered to excite the blood.

While spicy and often red in colour, dishes are not always that hot. A typical traditional meal includes *dal* (lentils), *bati* (baked wheat balls) and *churma* (powdered sweetened cereal). In the past, meat was a relative rarity, even amongst non-vegetarians, served in dishes such as the Maharaja of Salwar's *Junglee maas* (any meat from the hunt, cooked in pure ghee, salt and plenty of red chillies) or as *sulas* (marinated in pickles and grilled as kebabs). In Jaipur, Moghul traditions introduced richer *pulaos* and creamy dishes. Every district has its own sweets and desserts. The *Khansamas* (royal cooks) kept their recipes closely guarded secrets, handing them down through the palace kitchens. As many of these palaces are now hotels, tourists may have the good fortune to try them out.

BELOW *The chapatti production line doesn't seem quite so appealing when the temperature is soaring and you are working next to an open fire all day.*

TOP RIGHT *Supermarkets are still few and far between and grocery shopping means a trip down to the street market.*

BELOW RIGHT *Nuts and pulses are an essential part of a basically vegetarian diet, providing crucial proteins and carbohydrates at rock-bottom prices.*

LEFT *Tea (chai) is a vital part of Indian life, drunk hot, sweet and very milky.*

BELOW *A dozen different spices go into a basic garam masala. Every cook has their own carefully guarded recipe and always grinds their own spices.*

ABOVE *The colourful sabzi mandi (vegetable market) in Jaipur is well worth exploring for the atmosphere and photographic possibilities, even if you have nowhere to cook.*

RIGHT *Food at the street stalls can be delicious, as long as you watch it being cooked and can make sure it is hygienic.*

PEOPLE

If the countryside and the architecture of Rajasthan are beautiful, they only serve to frame its truly dazzling people. These are desert dwellers, with upright stance, chiselled features, piercing eyes and gleaming smiles. Flowing locks, moustaches and beards, and intricately wound turbans add colour and panache to the men. Saris of lime green and canary yellow, fuschia pink and scarlet turn the women into rainbows. Age and weather add canyons of experience. Every face is photogenic, every pair of deepset eyes has a story to tell. It may not be a pretty one: life here is not easy. Caste status is still highly relevant in Rajasthan, probably the most traditional and certainly one of the poorest states in India. Your caste is determined by birth and has nothing to do with wealth or upbringing, but in addition to the rigours of the caste system come class and money and deep divisions between the town and country, with tribal peoples, here before the arrival of the Rajputs, at the very bottom of the social pecking order. If you have high status you live as a god; lower down the line you have no rights and work around the clock.

BELOW *A Bhil tribal girl at Jaisamand Lake, near Udaipur. Rajasthan is the most caste-conscious area of India but the desert tribal people are considered to be below caste status.*

RIGHT *A retainer at Meherangarh Fort, Jodhpur. His face may not be his fortune, but his splendid moustache and turban have ensured a long queue of people waiting to take his photo and tip generously for the privilege.*

LEFT *Moustaches are something to smile about in Rajasthan – the fuller the better. This man in Jaipur may not be a contendor for the coveted Mr Desert title, but his whiskers and helmet are still a fine sight.*

TOP *A group of men wearing turbans wait for the bus at Kelvara village, near Kumbhalgarh Fort in southern Rajasthan.*

RIGHT *With the hair covered, beards and moustaches are pampered and styled and even dyed – and in this case, parted and curled.*

TOP LEFT *Life is sociable at the bathing ghats, as the women flock together to bath themselves, their children and do their laundry.*

BELOW FAR LEFT *Women gather together for a public meeting, their clothes a giddily gorgeous riot of colour.*

BELOW NEAR LEFT *Women are the work horses of Rajasthan, carrying water, farming and even breaking rocks to make a living. Carrying loads on their heads is a high price to pay for their perfect deportment.*

RIGHT *Bhil tribal girls dressed in colourful ghagras and cholis at Jaisamand Lake, near Udaipur. The women are fiercely protected by their families and men have to pay high dowries to marry a Bhil woman (the opposite of the usual Indian bride price, paid out by her father).*

TOP LEFT *Looking to the future? Over 65 per cent of the population of India is under the age of 25 and India's status in the world is rising rapidly, but whether the benefits of modern technology will stretch as far as these rural children is doubtful.*

BELOW FAR LEFT *A smiling Bhil tribal woman with her son, at Jaisamand Lake, near Udaipur. He has a hard life to look forward to. The Bhil were semi-nomadic hunter-herders whose men had a reputation as ferocious warriors. As the modern world has forced them to settle, they have never fully adapted, scratching a living from herding and hunting.*

BELOW NEAR LEFT *Torn between childhood and adulthood, this girl in eastern Rajasthan was den mother to a group of children playing cricket with old branches, anxiously guarding the little ones and only occasionally forgetting her chores.*

RIGHT *Some children just instinctively know how to play up to the camera; others are torn between posing and eating, such as this little boy tucking into a roti, near Mandawa, Shekhawati.*

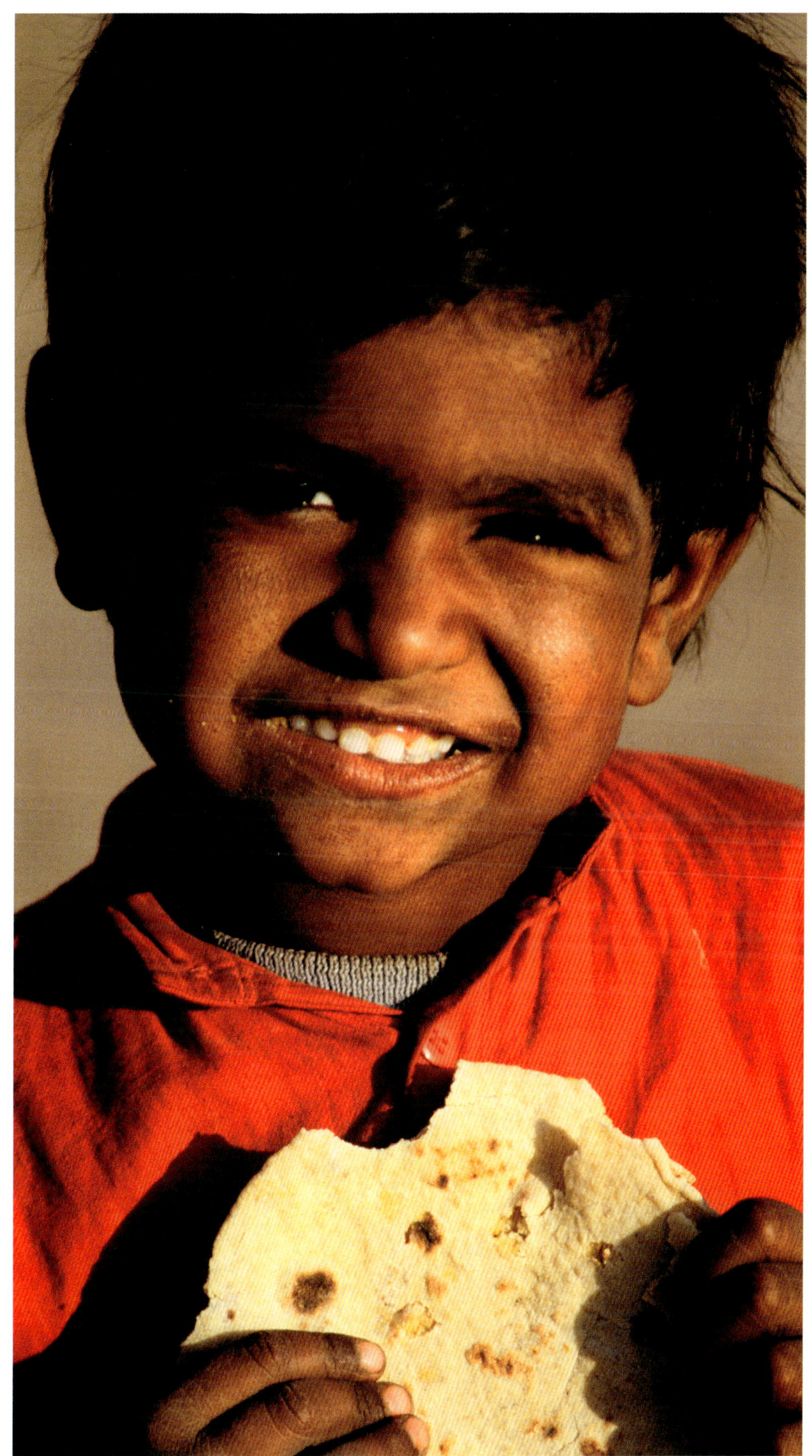

TOP LEFT *Women in Rajasthan will commonly cover their faces if men are around, using the scarf that comes as part of all types of traditional dress, whether the sari or shalwar kamiz.*

BELOW LEFT *Widows begging in a shady colonnade. It is the toughest of lives as a Rajasthani widow, with no means of support unless you have grown-up children willing to care for you.*

LEFT *Make-up and jewellery are all-important. Black kohl pencil lines the inner eye of even tiny babies, creating the dark, limpid eyes so typical of Indian women.*

BELOW *Everyone needs a little time out to read the paper, especially if you spend the rest of the day carving marble.*

OVERLEAF *Sari-wearing woman with baby and child, Jaipur. However poor, hot, overworked and put upon they are, women in Rajasthan seem to remain cool and beautiful at all times.*

RELIGION

Most people in Rajasthan are practicing Hindus, who believe in reincarnation and worship a vast pantheon of gods, all different aspects or incarnations of three major figures – Brahma (the Creator), Shiva (the Destroyer) and Vishnu (the Preserver). Jainism, a monastic, basically atheistic offshoot of Hinduism, founded in the 6th century BC, has a strong following here, especially amongst merchants and traders, while Islam was first introduced to the region in the 12th century AD. From the late 16th century, the influence of the Moghul court expanded the Muslim population, but was never sufficient to challenge the supremacy of Hinduism. There are also relatively small Sikh, Buddhist, Christian and Parsi communities.

LEFT *Fresh flowers, including marigolds, roses and jasmine, are regularly left as offerings at Hindu temples.*

BELOW *Stone carvings on a wall of the (Hindu) Sammidheshvar temple, Chittorgarh.*

RIGHT *Wandering Hindu sadhus (holy men) often lead extreme lives, living naked, covering themselves in ash or even walking on coals in their religious fervour.*

ABOVE AND FAR LEFT *Built by Rana Kumbha in 1439, Ranakpur, near Udaipur, is one of the five holiest places in the Jain religion and one of the most beautiful buildings in Rajasthan. It has 1,444 columns, each carved differently.*

LEFT *Jains are so conscious of the value of life that higher initiates will wear a scarf in case they inadvertently swallow a fly, and carry a small brush to clear ants out of their path.*

ABOVE *One of Rajasthan's more extraordinary sights. The Karni Mata Temple near Bikaner is dedicated to a 15th century mystic and is inhabited by sacred rats. It takes a great deal of willpower to take your shoes off before entering.*

LEFT *Karni Mata was so determined that death should not claim her devotees, that she decided they should all temporarily inhabit the bodies of rats. The temple rats are considered to hold the souls of all her tribe and are thus venerated and protected.*

LEFT *The lotus is a sacred flower in Hindu mythology, a symbol of purity, long life, health, honour and good luck. It is particularly associated with the goddess of wealth, Lakshmi.*

LEFT *Extraordinarily, this temple in Pushkar is one of only two in India dedicated to Lord Brahma, and the centre of a major pilgrimage during the Pushkar Mela each year.*

BELOW *The roof of the Brahma Temple Ghat, Pushkar. Although one of the holy trinity of the Hindu Pantheon, there are few temples to Brahma. He is said to have been self-born in the lotus flower that grows from the navel of Vishnu, is married to Saraswati, the goddess of learning and is traditionally depicted with four heads, four faces and four arms, riding a swan.*

जय श्री कृष्ण

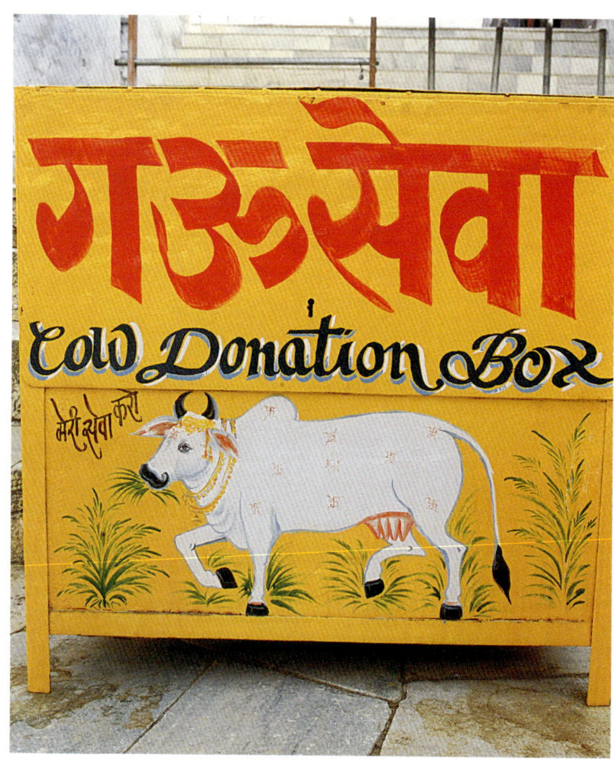
गऊसेवा
Cow Donation Box
मेरी सेवा करो

TOP LEFT *According to Hindu legend, the cow represents the mother goddess, a gift from the gods at the creation of the world.*

BELOW FAR LEFT *It is forbidden for a Hindu to kill, harm or impede a dairy cow and while they are owned and milked, they are free to wander and explore.*

BELOW NEAR LEFT *India has no social security, so alms and charity payments, fundamental to both Hindu and Muslim religious beliefs, are crucial to the survival of the poor. The sacred cow denotes a Hindu charity.*

TOP RIGHT *Kali the Goddess of Destruction has a surprisingly large and enthusiastic following, best known historically to the West in the thugee cult (origin of the word 'thug').*

BELOW RIGHT *The elegant stone statues we see today are not what was originally intended. Look closely and you can often see the last remnants of the paint that made the great temples as gaudy as this modern altar.*

FESTIVALS

As if there wasn't enough colour in Rajasthan, a year-round calendar of festivals and fairs helps to hype the atmosphere even further. Great religious festivals are celebrated with gusto. During Holi the air is thick with coloured dyes, while during Diwali the foundations shake from the firecrackers and candles that line the roads and railway tracks for the festival of lights. There are plenty of local religious festivals, too. Jaipur welcomes Makar Sankranti (the transition of the sun into the Northern hemisphere) with a riotous kite festival. Local women process images of Isar and Gangaur through the city during the Mewar Festival, which welcomes spring to Udaipur. Gauri, the consort of Lord Shiva, is revered by local women as the embodiment of conjugal love and marital fidelity. The Marwar Festival in Jodhpur commemorates the heroes of Rajasthan in music and dance, along with a camel tattoo show and polo. Pilgrimages are also turned into festivities.

Agricultural fairs and livestock markets such as the Pushkar Mela and the Bikaner Camel Market offer people in remote communities a chance to get out the glad rags, meet new people, catch up with the news and make a match for their daughters. Tented villages spring up amongst the cattle pens, wandering *fakirs* and musicians work the crowds. And then there are the tourist-led spectaculars such as the Jaipur Elephant Festival and Jaisalmer Desert Festival, with its moustache and bear competitions and camel races.

RIGHT *Holi is the Hindu Festival of Colour, observed on the first full moon in March each year to celebrate the harvest and fertility. The air is thick with bonfire smoke, marijuana and bombs of powdered dyes. Inhibitions are cast to the winds and the world is cleansed of evil spirits.*

TOP LEFT *Elephant processions, races and polo are huge draws at the Jaipur Elephant festival.*

BELOW LEFT *The twelve-day Pushkar Mela attracts over 100,000 locals, thousands of tourists and, according to Hindus, all 330 million Gods and Goddesses.*

BELOW RIGHT *This hand-pumped harmonium band were a popular attraction during Holi celebrations in a small village near Jaipur.*

RIGHT *The Pushkar Mela is also one of India's largest livestock markets, with thousands of cattle, camels, sheep and goats in the mêlée.*

STREET LIFE

It's burning under the sun between the blaring horns and traffic fumes, hot and airless in the dark windowless shops. Life is lived in the narrow bands of shade between the two, leapfrogging the open drains, the men lounging on the stepped pavements while the women cluster under the colonnades, shawls wrapped modestly across their faces. A group of small boys run beside the rickshaws, hands outstretched for rupees, rippling with laughter as they comment on the tourists in the safe knowledge they cannot be understood. A beggar woman suckles her baby in the shadow of a billboard advertising hair cream; another reaches out to stroke the arm of passersby in plaintive supplication. Three black, hairy pigs root through the gutters for scraps and a cow sits placidly chewing in the middle of the traffic, seemingly uncaring as cars swerve by. There is a big shady tree on the corner. Beside it, a kiosk with a pile of crates is doing a roaring trade in bottled water and fizzy drinks. A man sits cross-legged, mending bags and sewing on buttons, the tools of his trade laid out neatly on a cotton cloth. Nearby is another stall selling marigold garlands and candles to temple visitors. One man is asleep in the back of his rickshaw as he waits for customers; another walks past with a mattress on his head. Everywhere there is noise, dust, confusion, and exhilaration.

BELOW *Navigating a loaded camel cart through an overcrowded rural market requires some skill and a great deal of patience.*

ABOVE *Taking the lentils home for the lunchtime dal in backstreet Jaisalmer.*

RIGHT *It's always interesting to see how the other half lives.*

TOP LEFT *One mother to another – it's always sensible to be kind to animals if you believe in reincarnation. It could be one of your ancestors.*

BELOW LEFT *It's thirsty work, running a fast food stall – the open fire cooking the chef along with the food.*

ABOVE *Rooms are hot and airless, so much of life is lived in the open, from the barber to the dentist.*

RIGHT *A colourful sadhu sets up his stall in Udaipur with begging bowl and book.*

Shopping

There is an easy way to shop – at the government emporium which collects crafts from around the state and sells them to tour groups at set prices – but this isn't an authentic experience. Or you can try the various giant factory shops set up around the edges of the cities, where you can learn about carpets, jewellery and pottery in air-conditioned comfort. Alternatively, there are carpet and textile shops in ancient havelis where you perch on benches beneath carved galleries hung with luscious silks, and small shoemakers where you can watch as they hammer and stitch leather to fit your feet. Take time to wander in markets such as Johari Bazaar in Jaipur, with its bewitching alleys, piles of bangles and brass pots, and gleaming tomatoes and onions. Salesmen surround you, tugging at your sleeve – just one more deal, the first of the day, a good price for the lucky lady. Behind the bustle, in a heavily guarded backroom, local high society ladies have gathered to order new jewellery for a bride, picking over glittering heaps of diamonds and gold. Lac bangles and brass earrings are probably more in your price range, heaped high on market stalls, just waiting for you to start haggling.

FAR LEFT *Matkas (earthenware pots for storing water) and a letter box in Jaipur.*
BELOW LEFT *Pushkar is quiet for much of the year, the streets away from the temples and lakes a provincial market town, its shopkeepers sitting out the desert heat under shady awnings.*
LEFT *Take off your shoes, sit and drink tea while the fabrics are presented to you.*
BELOW *Once you have bought the cloth, take it down to the tailor for a fitting and he will make your garments to your own design.*
OVERLEAF *A young girl and her brother jump over a water-logged street in Fatehpur, Shekhawati.*

TRANSPORT

Few Indian trains have people sitting on the roof these days, though the rural buses certainly do. Then there are town buses, taxis, auto-rickshaws, bicycle rickshaws, private hire cars with a chauffeur, bicycles, mopeds, horse-drawn carriages, camels, elephants and horses. Or you could just walk! India has fabulous transport which comes in every possible guise. It is affordable and plentiful. It also requires guile, fortitude and patience to navigate. Booking a train or bus ticket can be a long-winded process; flagging down one of the vast fleet of busy little black and yellow auto-rickshaws in the cities will inevitably involve a lot of haggling, and sitting in a cycle rickshaw facing three lanes of oncoming rush hour traffic will probably lead to a feeling of utter helplessness and imminent doom. The frustrations are definitely outweighed by the possibilities of endless entertainment, however, even for the non-aficionado. The four-hour wait for an overdue train will pass in a flash of watching the cast of thousands, from the man running the tea stall to the family of beggars living on the platform. The streets are filled with donkey and camel carts, and the world really does seem a very long way down from an elephant's howdah.

BELOW *Elections are excitable occasions in India, with crowds of young men taking to the streets and waving flags from the backs of lorries. Astonishingly, with such fierce emotions and such a fragmented society, India's democratic traditions survive every upheaval.*

ABOVE *Mopeds are one of the most efficient ways to beat the traffic that builds up around Sanganeri Gate in Jaipur.*

RIGHT *Cycle rickshaws work only in the city centres and over relatively short distances. Most have given way to the ubiquitous black and yellow auto-rickshaw.*

ABOVE *The camel is so important to Rajasthan that the National Research Centre on Camels is based in Bikaner, breeding several different sub-species for heavy haulage or riding. The town also hosts a camel festival each January.*

LEFT *Air-conditioning is rudimentary on rural buses – few have any complete windows left and it is probably more comfortable on the roof, with three to a seat inside.*

RIGHT *Indian Railways are the largest national network in the world. They are slow and complicated to negotiate, but you can (eventually) get almost anywhere. The stations are a fascinating world, with everyone from brigadiers to beggars rubbing shoulders.*

BELOW LEFT *Check in your rearview mirror in Jaipur and don't be surprised if you see an elephant coming up on the inside. The city has plenty of working elephants.*

BELOW RIGHT *Railway porters are recognizable by their red jackets. Paying someone to carry your bags is one way to help spread tourist dollars to as many of the people as possible.*

Luxury Travel

If life is tough for the poor, the moneyed classes in India still live a life of seamless luxury barely contemplated by those in the West, with half-a-dozen servants, secretaries and other people to smooth their way through the bureaucracy and hassle. Pay for the privilege, and this courtesy is extended with a gracious smile to all visitors. You will be booked into magnificently restored former palaces where you will lie on canopied beds under painted ceilings, being waited on by the maharajah's family retainers. And while you cannot avoid the traffic-jams, you will enjoy the spectacle from a luxury air-conditioned car, with a chauffeur and a courier whose sole task is to make you happy. Or you can just book a trip on the Palace on Wheels, a fabulous eight-day rail tour of Rajasthan with luxurious modern carriages whose designs are based on those of the Rajput and Gujarat princes, the Nizam of Hyderabad and the Viceroy of British India.

ABOVE *Mewar State Railway was created by Maharana Fateh Singh (1884–1930) and incorporated into Indian Railways when Rajasthan joined the Union in 1955.*

BELOW LEFT *The Palace on Wheels is one of the world's most glamorous trains, with carriages based on the Maharajas' private trains and unsurpassed service.*

TOP RIGHT *India is one of the few places on the planet where the ordinary tourist can live like a queen. A chauffeur is positively recommended – few foreign drivers could brave the traffic safely. The Taj Lake Palace Hotel, Udaipur, provides the car, the chauffeur and the film star feeling.*

BELOW RIGHT *Guests of the Taj Lake Palace Hotel, Udaipur, take a boat trip fit for a goddess on Lake Pichola during the Gangaur Festival in Udaipur.*

RURAL LIFE

Water rules the rhythm of life in rural Rajasthan. Those lucky enough to live near a river or tank husband its resources through the long dry months. The rest survive on next to nothing, using sand to scrub their pots, bathing in a cupful of water and drinking buttermilk, making the long, hot journey across the sand to fill their pots. Houses are built from the local earth, round adobe huts with thatched roofs, the walls plastered, decorated and termite-proofed with a blend of clay, cow-dung and hay, or painstakingly built from sun-dried bricks. This, like so many other things here, is the role of the women, who cook over an open stove, fuelled by wood or dried cattle dung. They live a life almost entirely segregated from men, although the community is tightly knit, sharing good times and bad, and punishing transgressors in village courts. Villagers are largely self-sufficient, creating pots and baskets, making and embroidering their own clothes and herding cattle, sheep, camels and goats. People who live so close to the whims of nature are always respectful of the gods – every house has a shrine. Amongst the rural communities, many are nature-worshipping Bishnois, self-appointed guardians of the nation's wildlife. Others include the Bhil, Mina and Sariyal tribes who were here before the Rajputs arrived.

BELOW *The end of a hard day on a camel trek – they may seem benign, but hours in a camel saddle can be close to torture for the first few years.*

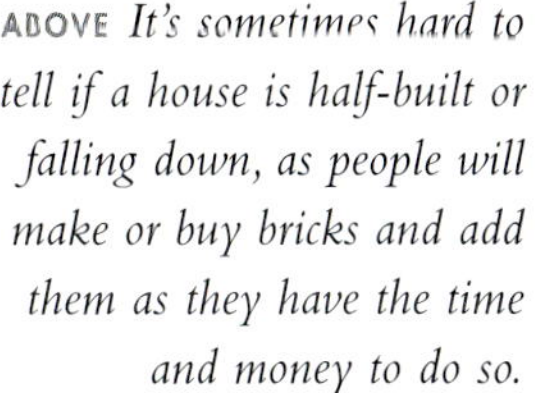

ABOVE *It's sometimes hard to tell if a house is half-built or falling down, as people will make or buy bricks and add them as they have the time and money to do so.*

RIGHT *The money that tourists bring to the desert has proved a lifeline for many remote communities, and a camel trek is an experience never to be forgotten.*

OVERLEAF *A rural bus stop with the men and women waiting in separate sections. The buses also always have a ladies' section, and no man may sit there unless invited by a female companion.*

P 43
10/11/03

LEFT *With no fans, air-conditioning or even roofs, and burning desert heat, shade is a precious commodity in the desert villages.*

BELOW *Waiting for a bus – patience is an Indian art form, and while the queue may not be orderly, the long wait for overdue transport is a time to catch up with gossip.*

ABOVE *However poor they are and dusty their surroundings, the Rajasthani women manage to look elegant, their beautiful saris vivid against the sand.*

RIGHT *Men and animals snatch food and water where they can, but there is rarely sufficient to cover their ribs.*

THE NATURAL WORLD

Rajasthan is a desert state, a land of gold sand and scrub thorns where men in turbans lead camels through the dunes. But it is also a land of lakes and mountains, where water cascades through the folds of the Aravalli Hills and collects in mirror-clear indigo-dark basins, where tigers slink through the forests and herons perch, still as statues, in the reeds of swamps. It has never been a forgiving land. Life is not easy for any of its inhabitants, human, animal or vegetable. But the harsh reality has preserved its beauty. This is still India and you are never far from villages, but there are vast swathes of Rajasthan that are still remote and undeveloped, with hills, dunes and forests ripe for exploration under the glorious clear afternoon light and night skies carpeted with stars.

BELOW *One of the most beautiful and holy places in Rajasthan, Pushkar Lake is said to have been created when Lord Brahma dropped a lotus flower.*

ABOVE *The crenellated walls of Kumbhalgarh Fort stretch some 36 km (22 miles) across the Aravalli Hills, an ancient mountain range which stretches eastwards across India for 500 km (300 miles).*

LEFT *Little of the Thar Desert is empty sand dunes; most is covered in scrub which needs only the tiniest drop of rain to burst into flower and fruit.*

The Great Thar Desert

Some time around 5–10,000 years ago, tectonic plates shifted, drying up the Ghaggar River and creating the vast Thar desert basin, which covers around 238,700 sq km (93,000 sq miles) in Rajasthan, southern Haryana and Punjab, extending across the India border into Pakistan. It is bordered by the Indus River, the Aravalli Hills, the Arabian Sea and the Punjab plain. There are areas of shifting sands where waves of dunes up to 150 m (492 ft) high ripple wind-blown across the plains, but much of the region is made up of low, rocky ground and scrubby vegetation that clings to life thanks to around 25 cm (10 in) of rain a year. Canals in the north and west have reclaimed some of the land for agriculture and there are some lakes, but little of the desert can be farmed. Villagers, mainly either Bhil or Bishnoi tribal people, survive as cattle and goat herders, living a poverty-stricken existence in mud and thatch homes, largely forgotten by the outside world.

Surprisingly, the harsh environment supports a wide range of wildlife, with 23 species of lizard and 25 species of snake inhabiting the dunes, while larger species including the black buck, Indian wild ass, great Indian bustard and several species of eagle are commonly seen in the Desert National Park near Jaisalmer.

ABOVE *Many desert women still have to walk miles each day to fetch water, balancing the precious pots on their heads.*

LEFT *Turbans laid out to dry under the desert sun.*

RIGHT *Camels provide transport, milk, wool and meat, and their broad padded feet are still one of the most efficient ways of travelling on sand.*

Animal Life

Everyone associates India with elephants and tigers, but it is actually home to over 500 species of mammal, including elusive Asian leopards, sloth bears and striped hyenas and over 2,000 species of bird, from the national symbol, the peacock, to the great flocks of green parakeets that chatter in every city garden. Sambar deer, chital, nilgai and black bucks graze in the bush, water buffaloes lounge in the shallows, monkeys loop through the branches and small animals such as mongooses, porcupines and ground squirrels scuttle through the undergrowth.

Rajasthan is lucky enough to have three of the country's finest wildlife reserves: Ranthambore National Park, which has tigers, Keoladeo Ghana National Park near Bharatpur, which is a world-class bird sanctuary, and Sariska National Park. Pristine desert is preserved in the vast Desert National Park near Jaisalmer. These precious oases are a magical world away from the crush of humanity in the Indian cities, a slower, quieter, more peaceful world, where the loudest noise is the crackle of a twig or the rustle of deer as it tears a mouthful of fresh grass.

TOP LEFT *Who's checking out who? The urban monkeys enjoy people-watching.*
FAR LEFT *When a peacock spreads its tail here, it is said that rain is on its way.*
NEAR LEFT *Sambar deer grow up to 300 kg (663 lbs), with antlers up to 1 m (3 ft) long.*
ABOVE *The water hole at the Shikarbadi, a former hunting lodge in Udaipur.*
LEFT *Water buffalo wait out the midday heat.*

Tigers

The Royal Bengal tiger is the largest cat in the world (over 2 m/6.5 ft long), with a rich amber coat striped with black and brown and white underparts. Tigers are solitary, territorial and highly defensive. Females will range an area of around 20 sq km (8 sq miles), while males can roam anything from 60–100 sq km (23–39 sq miles). They are effective but not enthusiastic hunters and prefer larger prey such as sambar or wild boar which they will store, returning to the carcass for several days. A female will rear her brood of three to four cubs on her own. They will leave their mother at about 30 months old and reach sexual maturity a year to 18 months later.

In 1972, with numbers reaching critically low proportions, the Indian government launched Project Tiger, a programme of protection and education that has created huge forest reserves and tried, with limited success, to tackle poaching. Today, around half of the roughly 6,000 tigers that survive in the wild are in India, around 1,000 of those in Project Tiger reserves such as Ranthambore. Even here, although heavily protected, they are not immune from poaching. Sariska, in northern Rajasthan, had tigers until recently, but they haven't been seen here for several years. Without tourists, the tiger would have died out long ago.

ABOVE *Pavilions built for human hunters are also useful for the four-footed variety, offering shade and a perfect view.*

LEFT *Even tigers can be cute and cuddly, rolling on their backs like domestic kittens, although tickling their tummy could be foolhardy. An adult male can weigh upwards of 300 kg (663 lbs) and even with claws sheathed, paws the size of a dinner plate could break a person's neck with one swipe.*

RIGHT *The orange and black stripes can provide strikingly effective camouflage for a hungry tiger.*

OVERLEAF *Dawn rises over the Aravalli Hills near Jaipur.*

FOLLOWING PAGES *A sarangi player follows the tourists up to serenade the sunset over Jaisalmer.*

INDEX

Italicised entries indicate photographs.

PHOTOGRAPHIC CREDITS

The author and L & L Media would like to thank the following for their help: Cox and Kings, www.coxandkings.co.uk; The Indian Tourist Office, www.incredibleindia.org; Karoki Lewis, www.karokilewis.com; Taj Hotels, Resorts and Palaces, www.tajhotels.com.

The following photographs were taken by Karoki Lewis, Photograph © Karoki Lewis: front cover, 1, 2–3, 6–7, 10, 11, 15 (t), 17 (t), 19 (b), 23, 24–25, 27 (b), 31, 32, 33, 41, 43 (t), 44–45, 50-51, 52, 53 (t), 55, 57 (r), 60 (t), 61, 69 (t), 70, 72, 73 (t), 75, 76 (bl), 77, 79 (b), 80-81, 82 (b), 88 (br), 96 (b), 98 (t), 99 (b) , 100–101, 110–111, 115 (t), 121, 122–23, 124–125.

All other photographers and/or their agents are credited below.

Key to locations: t = top; b = bottom; l = left; r = right; tr = top right; br = bottom right. (No abbreviation is given for pages with a single image, or pages on which all photographs are by the same photographer.)

CK Cox and Kings
CW Carol Wright
DM Duncan Mills
GMB Gillian Muller von Blumencron
ITO India Tourist Office
JG Jennifer Gilmour
JR John Ruler
KL Karoki Lewis, Photograph © Karoki Lewis
LY Lisa Young
MJ Mary Johns
MJS Melissa Shales
RS Reuben Steains
SB Steve Bailey
SK Sudha Kaviraj
SV Sunil Vaidyanathan
TH Taj Hotels, Resorts and Palaces
TWG Tony Waltham Geopictures

Endpapers		MJS	48		MJS	76	br	MJS	103	t	MJS
Back cover, left to right		MJS ,	49	t	TH	78	t	TWG	103	b	GVB
ITO, CK, MJS, MJS			49	b	MJS	78	b	SV	104	t	RS
Inside front flap		MJS	53	b	MJS	79	t	MJS	104	b	JG
4–5		ITO	54		CK	82	t	JR	105	t	MJS
8–9		RS	56		MJS	83		RS	105	bl	SK
12–13		SV	57	l	CK	84	t	CK	106	t	CW
14		MJS	58	t	JG	84	bl	CW	105	br	SB
15	b	RS	58	b	CW	84	br	MJS	106	b	JG
16		MJS	59	t	MJS	85		SV	107		TH
17	b	JG	59	b	JG	86	t	SV	108		JR
19	t	GMB	60	b	MJS	86	b	RS	109	t	MJS
20–21		SV	62		SV	87	b	RS	109	b	SV
22		MJS	63	t	ITO	88	bl	CK	110-111		KL
26	t	JG	63	b	MJS	89		MJS	112	t	JG
26	bl	MJS	64		JG	90-91		ITO	112	b	MJS
26	br	DM	65	t	RS	92	t	CK	113		JG
27	t	JG	65	b	TH	92	bl	MJS	114		RS
28–29		CK	66		CW	92	br	TWG	115	b	MJS
30		TH	67		JG	93		MJS	116-117		ITO
34–35		LY	68	t	CW	94		JG	116	bl	TWG
36–37		SV	68	b	RS	95	t	JG	116	r	RS
38		MJS	69	b	JR	95	b	CK	117	b	RS
39		TWG	71		MJS	96	t	JG	118	t	DM
40		DM	73	b	SV	97	t	RS	118	bl	MJS
42		MJS	74	t	GVB	97	b	TWG	118	br	JG
43	bl	MJS	74	bl	SV	98	b	MJS	119	t	MJ
43	br	JG	74	br	GVB	99	t	TWG	119	b	MJS
46-47		SV	76	t	SV	102		LY	120		ITO

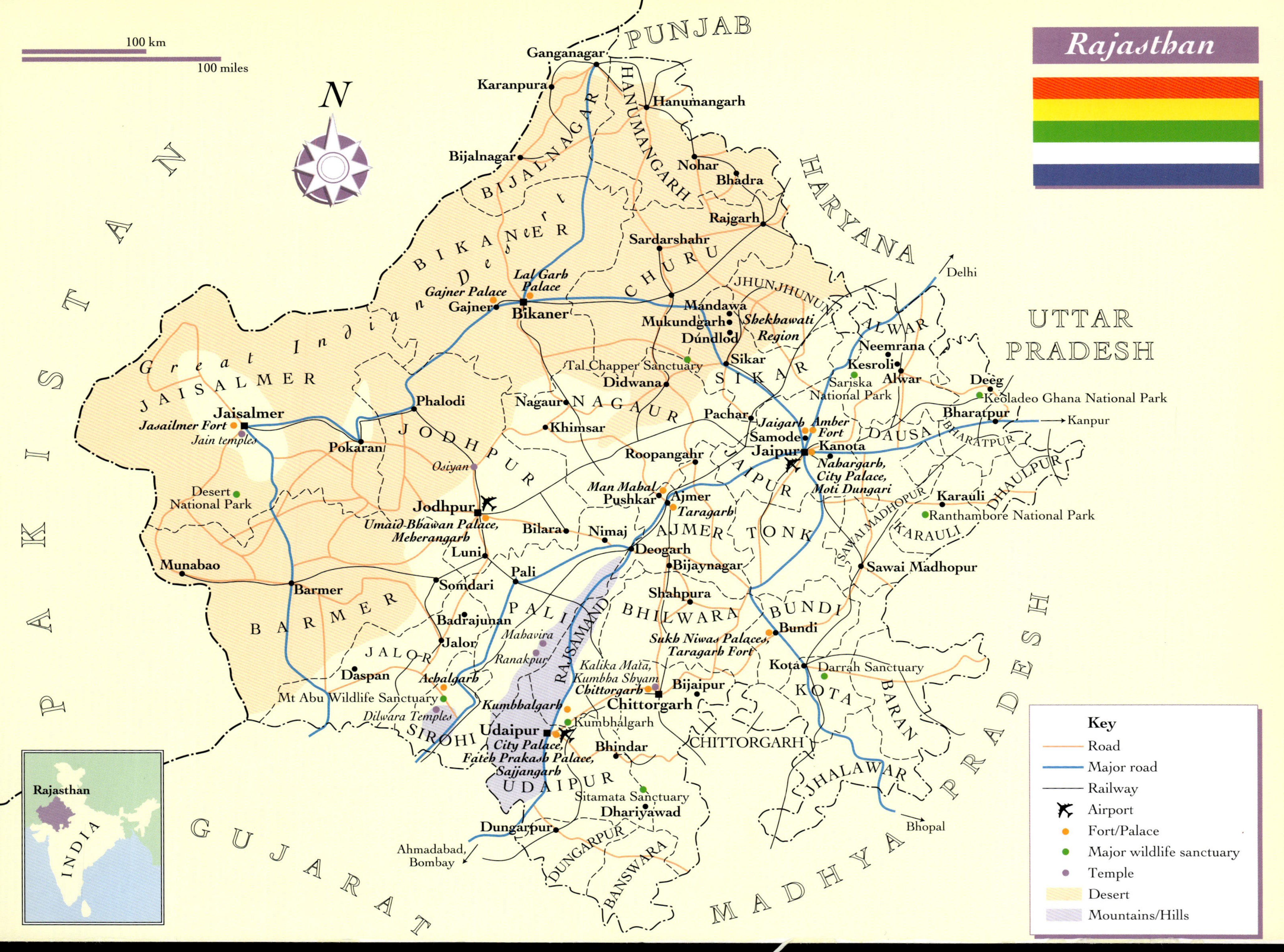

Rajasthan
100 km
100 miles
N
PUNJAB
HARYANA
UTTAR PRADESH
MADHYA PRADESH
GUJARAT
PAKISTAN
Great Indian Desert
Ganganagar
Karanpura
Hanumangarh
HANUMANGARH
Bijalnagar
BIJALNAGAR
Nohar
Bhadra
Rajgarh
Sardarshahr
CHURU
BIKANER
Lal Garh Palace
Gajner Palace
Gajner
Bikaner
JHUNJHUNUN
Mandawa
Mukundgarh
Dundlod
Shekhawati Region
Sikar
SIKAR
Tal Chapper Sanctuary
Didwana
Nagaur
NAGAUR
Khimsar
JAISALMER
Jaisalmer
Jasailmer Fort
Jain temples
Pokaran
Phalodi
JODHPUR
Osiyan
Desert National Park
Jodhpur
Umaid Bhawan Palace, Meherangarh
Bilara
Nimaj
Luni
Munabao
Barmer
BARMER
Somdari
Pali
PALI
Badrajunan
Jalor
JALOR
Daspan
Achalgarh
Mt Abu Wildlife Sanctuary
Dilwara Temples
SIROHI
Mahavira
Ranakpur
RAJSAMAND
Kumbhalgarh
Udaipur
City Palace, Fateh Prakash Palace, Sajjangarh
UDAIPUR
Dungarpur
DUNGARPUR
BANSWARA
Ahmadabad, Bombay
Sitamata Sanctuary
Dhariyawad
Bhindar
Chittorgarh
CHITTORGARH
Kalika Mata, Kumbha Shyam Chittorgarh
Bijaipur
Sukh Niwas Palaces, Taragarh Fort
Bundi
BUNDI
Kota
KOTA
Darrah Sanctuary
BARAN
JHALAWAR
Bhopal
BHILWARA
Shahpura
Bijaynagar
Deogarh
AJMER
TONK
Man Mahal
Pushkar
Ajmer
Taragarh
Roopangahr
Pachar
Jaigarh
Amber Fort
Samode
Jaipur
JAIPUR
Kanota
Nahargarh, City Palace, Moti Dungari
ALWAR
Neemrana
Kesroli
Alwar
Sariska National Park
Delhi
Deeg
Keoladeo Ghana National Park
Bharatpur
BHARATPUR
Kanpur
DAUSA
DHAULPUR
Karauli
KARAULI
Ranthambore National Park
SAWAI MADHOPUR
Sawai Madhopur
Rajasthan
INDIA
Key
Road
Major road
Railway
Airport
Fort/Palace
Major wildlife sanctuary
Temple
Desert
Mountains/Hills